AF130122

Karolina Plachetko

The Book of Scents

Prose - Poetry - Photographs

Bibliographische Information der Deutschen Nationalbibliothek:
Die Deutsche Nationalbibliothek verzeichnet diese Publikation
in der Deutschen Nationalbibliographie; detaillierte bibliographische
Daten sind im Internet unter http://dnb.dnb.de abrufbar.

Herstellung und Verlag:

BoD – Books on Demand, Norderstedt

ISBN: 978-3-7357-9338-6

for those I love[d]

Offerings

This is what I am:
not
fragile, pure, or decent,
but
ravished, torn, abandoned.

And by accepting
the offer,
you will never get
the extras,
nor the special bargains.

A look into my soul
will burn your sight.
The touch of my waist
will crush your knuckles.
My kiss
will certainly and inescapably
drown you.

Fatal is what I am.

And fatal is all there is.

                          - Karolina Plschetko

The true self of an artist

What I am not.
A photographer. A writer.
A singer. A lover.

What I wish I ~~were~~ were.
A photographer. A writer.
A singer. A lover.

What I actually am.
A mother.
And long ago, a wife.

                    - Karolina Plachetko

LUFTPOST
PAR AVION
PRIORITAIRE

The Laughter

Your laughter in my hand
when I tell you
to be a little more silent.

Your kisses on my fingertips
as you refuse
to be silent at all.

— Karolina Plachetko

7.00 Little Thought

7.30

8.00 ~~Go ahead little thought, tell me the~~
8.30 ~~story that lies under your paper.~~

9.00

9.30 No, don't fool me with lines,
10.00 don't fool me with names.

10.30 ~~Go deep down, straight down into the~~
11.00 ~~center.~~

11.30

12.00 Show me your filth, your horror,
12.30 your crime, show me everything broken.

13.00
13.30 ~~I want to know your every detail, your~~
~~every fear, and all the pictures~~
14.00 ~~you hide from the morning,~~
14.30

15.00 Just let me see how much I can take
15.30 and how much I can stand before wisdom
16.00 will force me to alter.

16.30
17.00 ~~And then, when it is done, when all~~
~~damage proclaims and we rest naked, in~~
17.30 ~~silence, one next to the other,~~
18.00 no comfort will harm what no pleasure
18.30 can hide in the truth of your little
~~torture.~~
19.00

19.30

20.00

20.30   Wichtig
21.00   — Karolina Plachetko

21.30

22.00

Precious and fragile things

Can I ask you something?
Can I teach you life?
You smile back tears.
A bowl of chicken soup will do,
so you say,
with ginger and your mother's
spices.
Of course, I reply, but I miss you.
Don't worry, you say,
don't waste your precious time
on melancholy,
take u a walk, look around,
smell the air,
it is fragile but it's pure.
Yes, it is, i say,
but your hands are empty,
your smile a fake.

                    - Karolina Plachetko

Breathless

We listened to Cat Power's
Breathless.
The sun didn't rise that
morning.
But we didn't care.
Nothing was new.
Nothing was veiled.
Everything was easy.
We followed each other's
steams and mists.
Our voices melted silently.
You loved me then.
And I dind't ask for more.

                    - Karolina Plachetko

HOT WHITE WALLS, BLACK SHADOWS..THE AROMA OF STRANGE
EASTERN SPICES, BAZAAR DELIGHTS! THE SCENT OF SANDALWOOD
AND CLOVES. A SOUND OF LAUGHTER AND MUSIC AND DRUMS...

Prelude

Old man, what have I done to
deserve this?
Your prologue of sageness and
maturity bores me.
Your arrangements and schemes
are a burden and not a relief.
But yes, I am too young and
my heart is too wild to follow
your old-fashioned rules of
attraction.

Does age really matter when it
comes to the silence under your
skin?
The silence, the whisper, the
famine?

Your skin does not bother.
But you do.

                    - Karolina Plachetko

Breath

Breathe me slowly, take me in.
What may come, may come, let us
begin.
Let's go back to where everything
starts, without the truth
of an ending.
Where passion is not only a word
and love in her unprepared ways
unpretending.

Unleashed and unbound your desire
will enter, will meet mine down in
the hall.
Completely defeated, overwhelmed by
the beauty, leading the path to
surrender.

No word will bee spoken,
no song will be sung,
only the thrill of each other naked.
Pawing the ground, crawling under
the surface.

Then you will breathe me while I'll
be seeking asylum.
You will hold me and touch me and
watch.
I will love you while breaking free
from your silence.
I will let you and make you,
it starts.

                    - Karolina Plachetko

The Embrace

Yes, it is your voice. Your old
and gentle voice that keeps me
here where I don't belong in the
first place. Obviously I don't
do that because my life is so
much more different from the
moment you create within the
vibration of your larynx.

Sometimes I ask you random things
only to hear you talk, and
sometimes I'm afraid of asking
you to read out loud a few
pages of your favorite book, in
case you could decipher my
thoughts and expose them to the
air around us where they no
longer remain silent and hidden,
where I no longer can conseal
myself from you completely. For
I need to hide every now and
then, especially when we meet,
precisely when we meet.

When it rains I imagine us sitting
on the white staircase in your
house, the rooms all empty with
light, only filled with the
sound of rain drops against the
window ae panes. Then, suddenly,
your voice melts into this moment
of silence, its used and broken
sonority, at first almost
struggling with the soundless
space between us, but becoming
wiser and stronger, defiant with
every new word, with every new
thought, like an angry whisper
sometimes, thus honest and calm.

Sometimes I imagine us visiting
a foreign country or city. In my
thoughts it is always summer then,
hot enough to feel ashamed, cool
enough to feel secure. For a long
time we simply walk through the
streets and alleys, look into the
shop windows, watch the strangers
passing by. And then you begin
to invent stories for me, weaving
in the faces of the people we meet
or the houses we see, the dishes
we taste.

-2-

Your voice like an old sailor
then, experienced, excited and hum-
ble, like the shabby chic of
old-fashioned furniture at the
flea market.

I always fall for that, for your
voice, you know. I can't help it
and I suppose I never will. You
enfold me with its sound and
tuneless melody like other people
enfold their children, parents,
lovers. I am too much yours and
too less mine then, and I like
that condition of not being
forced to be myself and to act all
rational and grown-up.

It is your voice.

                    - Karolina Plachetko

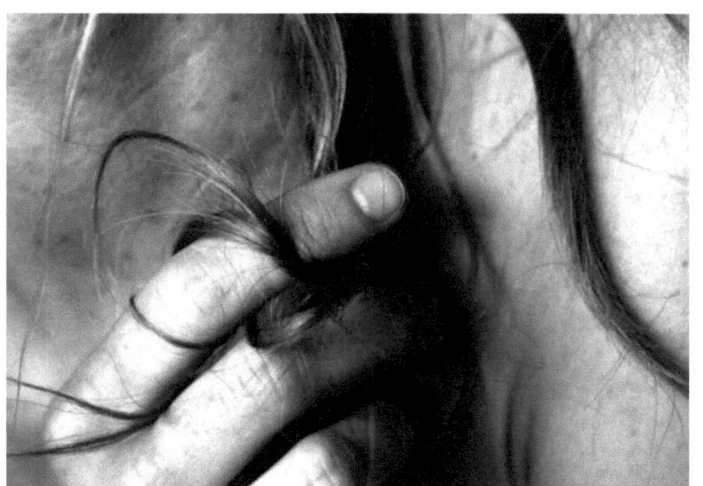

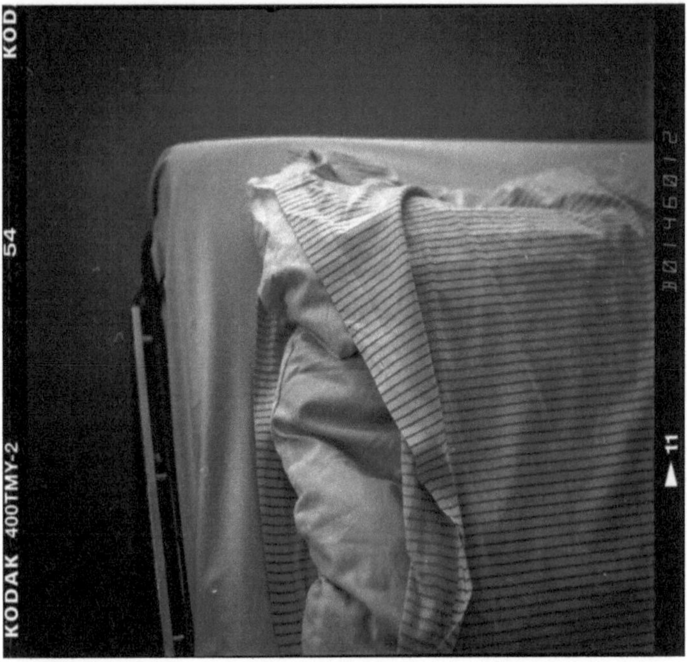
KODAK 400TMY-2
54
KOD
11

Epiphany

Something went wrong.

We did.

— Karolina Plachetko

About the
significance of
insignificance

LUFTPOST
PAR AVION
PRIORITAIRE

Who am I to tell you
about the insignificance
of this or that?
It is, in fact, what you see
and therefore I should
respect and appreciate your
courage to tell me
all about it.
Seriously, I should do that.
So bring it on –
and don't dare to leave out
all the boring parts like,
"I woke up this morning",
and,
"My eyelid is twitching".

          – Karolina Plachetko

The Dead Prostitute

my hair has grown cold from
the morning
so please go on and decipher
my skin
try not to hesitate with the
fractured bruises and shins

sometimes we do not possess
enough time
to clean the room or to
straighten out everything
frayed
and since the virtues we
transgress pass into oblivion
it is important to keep
the pace humble
and to repent to the
so-called healing of wounds

                    — Karolina Plachetko

Luftpost
Air Mail
Par Avion

Ink

I want to go home,
to my old typewriter
and my old paper,
the blue air mail envelopes,
the scent of my
grandfather's thoughts,
and the ink,
the black,
the red ink.
I want to go home so badly.
So badly.

— Karolina Plachetko

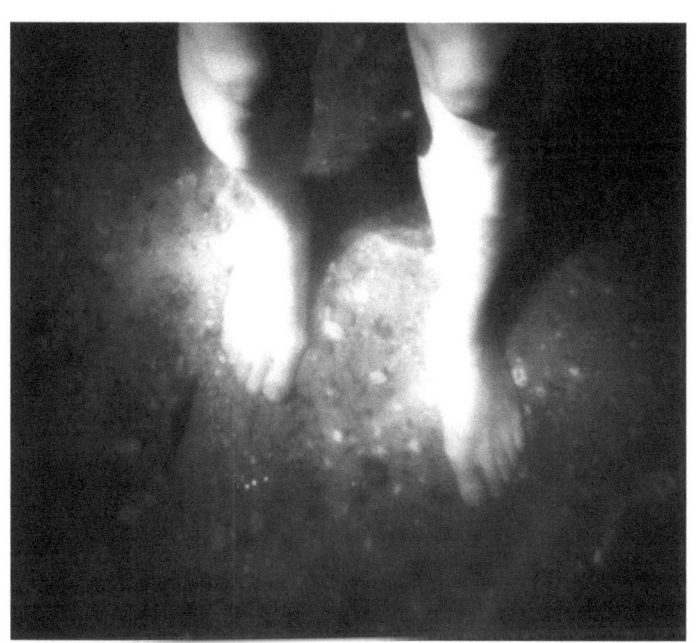

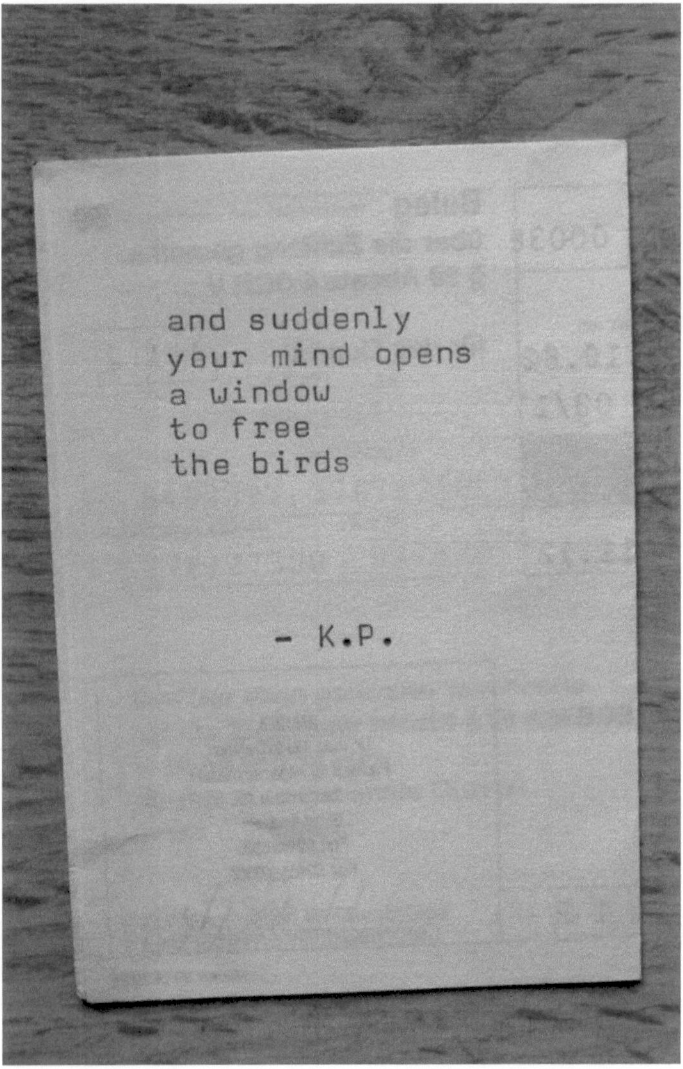

and suddenly
your mind opens
a window
to free
the birds

        - K.P.

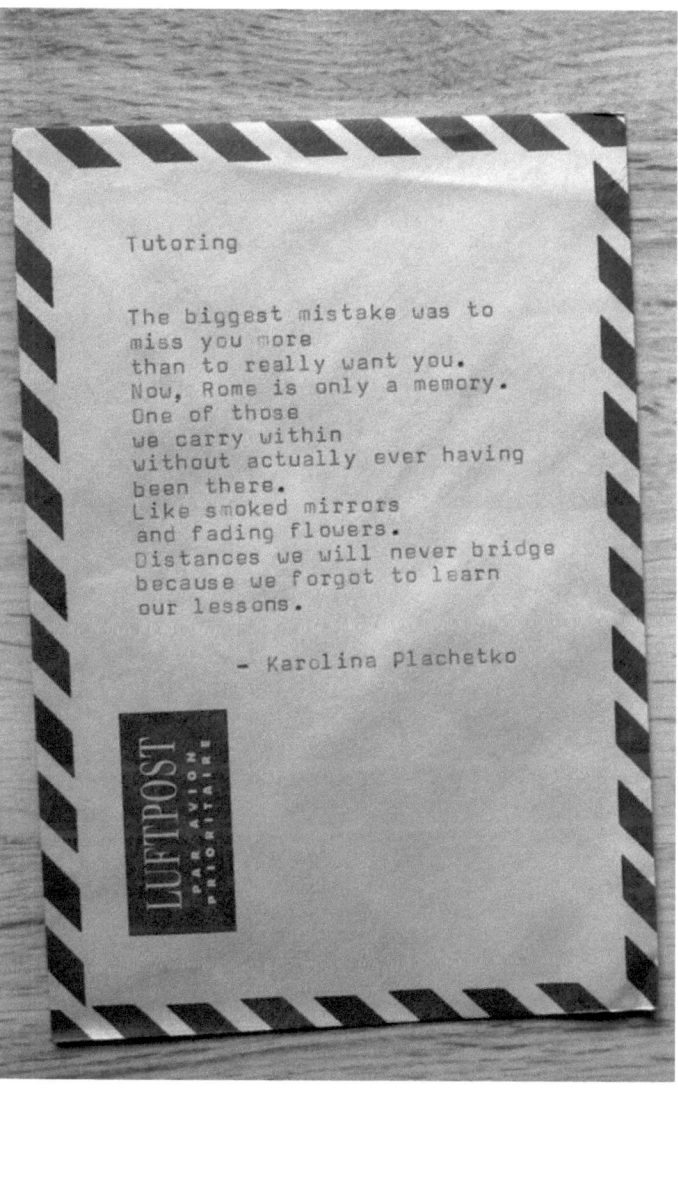

Tutoring

The biggest mistake was to
miss you more
than to really want you.
Now, Rome is only a memory.
One of those
we carry within
without actually ever having
been there.
Like smoked mirrors
and fading flowers.
Distances we will never bridge
because we forgot to learn
our lessons.

— Karolina Plachetko

LUFTPOST
PAR AVION
PRIORITAIRE

Unexpected

I wake up in the morning
and look outside the window.
With the sleep in my hair
and a bad taste in my mouth,
I'm afraid it was all just
a dream.

The promises, the plans,
the unexpected.
Your tongue, your skin,
your hand between my thighs,
my smile.

With a blurry face
I gaze upon the sheets.

They are pleated, plain and
empty.

                    — Karolina Plachetko

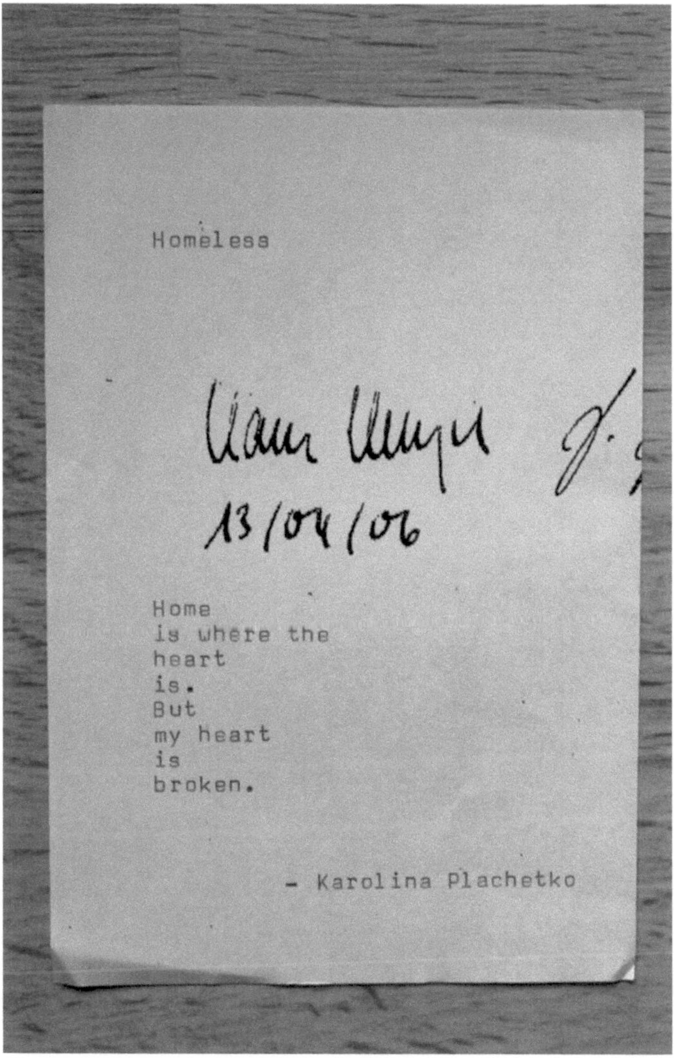

Homeless

[signature]
13/04/06

Home
is where the
heart
is.
But
my heart
is
broken.

        — Karolina Plachetko

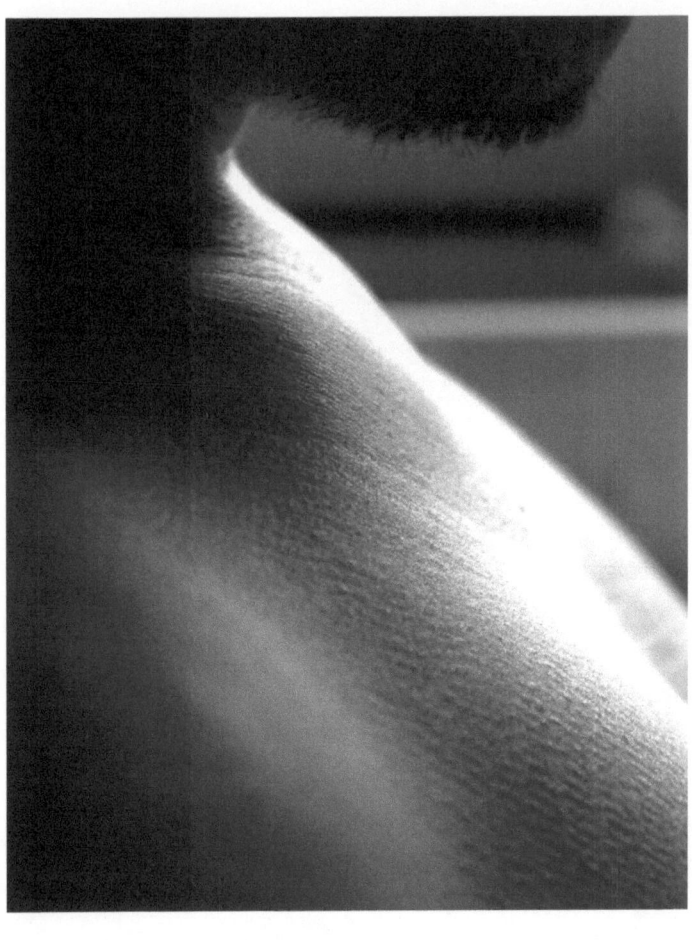

The Moth

Here I am again, in the darkness
of my room. The city went to bed,
one by one the lights got out, and
silence took over. She always does,
with her dreams and her desires,
with the fading light and the night
hawks coming to life again. Like
lost moths they flutter around the
street lights, burning their wings
to the heated bulbs, unable to
learn and to fly away. They are
bound by what they cannot have,
being trapped by the things that
will certainly kill them.

Once I had a tea light with a
drowned moth inside the wax. And
the shape of its wings was per-
fectly clear, like a scientific draw
drawing in a nature study book.
The poor thing fele fell for the
flame and never escaped.

I often held the tea light in my
hand and I looked at the conserved
creature with both amazement and
compassion, and I wondered how

-1-

cruel nature can be. And yet, how
beautiful in her cruelty.

I gave that tea light away to some-
one I thought would take perfect ~~ee~~
care of it, along with a shell and
the sound of music. But you know
how it is with those things we
give away. Some of them get lost,
others stolen, and a few simply
disappear. In the end I never saw
my moth again, neither did I ~~dee~~
see the shell, nor heard its
music. Only the memory of them
remained, and so I sometimes
catch myself thinking about those
items I once have possessed. You
would have held it in your hand
and watched it carefully, studying
the perfection of the wax and the
wings and the moment. Vanitas.
More beautiful than any artist
could have captured it.

You would have liked that fragile,
wasted part of me.   -2-

- Karolina Plachetko

The Dancing Room

The day you no longer will be
part of my life, i will start
learning to play the piano.
The chords, the melodies, my
fingers upon the black and the
white, turning my mind, dancing
with my hands the way you once
danced with me.

Do you remember?

But our dancing room will remain
empty.The trees will fade into
the falling night. i will have my
debut at two thirty in the
morning, when all the other dancers
will go to sleep,
silently waiting to forget.

                    - Karolina Plachetko

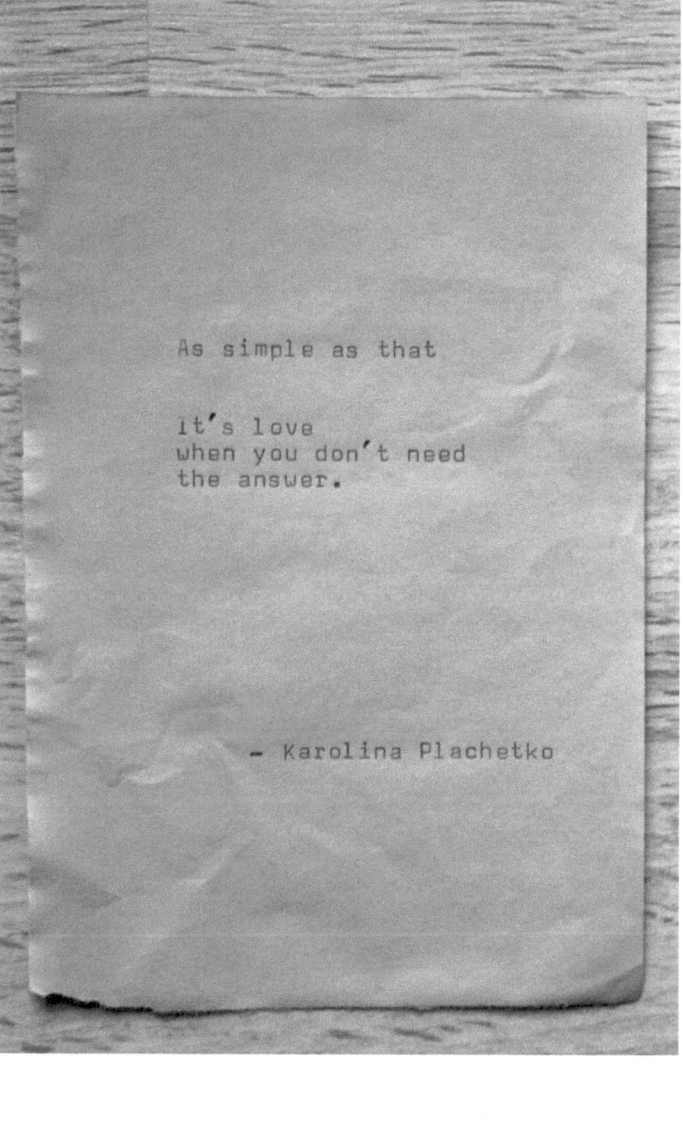

As simple as that

it's love
when you don't need
the answer.

                  - Karolina Plachetko

In Between

Hold me so close now
I can hear your heart and your
skin
softly correspond
with the gulping and bulging
sound of my blood

Don't try to fix
what nature so bravely
managed to leave broken for
decades
it is, so far, not your fault
therefore, you're not in the
position
to decide or to decalre

Only to feel and to be certain
about the undemanding
unpredictable
and current
alliance of these two bodies
briefly connecting at your door

                    — Karolina Plachetko

Polyamory

In the simplicity of thoughts
we cannot blind out the distance.

Feelings come and go,
they bind, they suffer.

On your skin
the fragile scent of being
human.

Within my hair
the fragrance of sobriety.

Above all
the nakedness of morning.

                    - Karolina Plachetko

The scent of your skin

Slowly the day falls asleep.
And slowly the night wakes up too.
The scent of your obsolete skin
and of soap,
drenched in the shadows of longing.

Like memories you barely remember,
and like memories you cannot
forget,
you move through the darkening city
with the pigeons lost in their
grey.

Your flaws, your mistakes,
and your trembling,
soften like moso in your hand.
Your sight silently falters
and dances,
until,
with the first shadows of rain,
your costume of true blissful
meanings
slowly seasons away.

                    - Karolina Plachetko

Trans-Siberian

Travel with me around the
world.
From your navel to my cheek
bones.
Let us find those places
carefully and secretly
hidden by time.
Beads of sweat dripping
down your skin.
Flowers in my hair.
Give me a good night kiss
with the first glimpse of a
September morning,
in the economy class
compartment of the
Trans-Siberian Railway
on its route to China.

                    - Karolina Plachetko

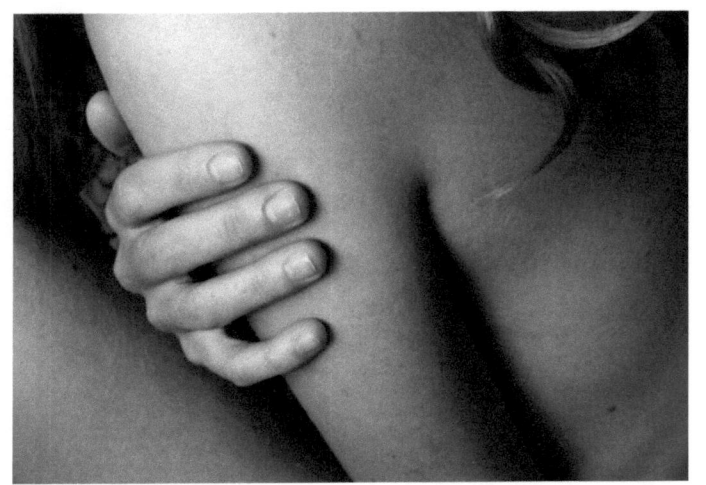

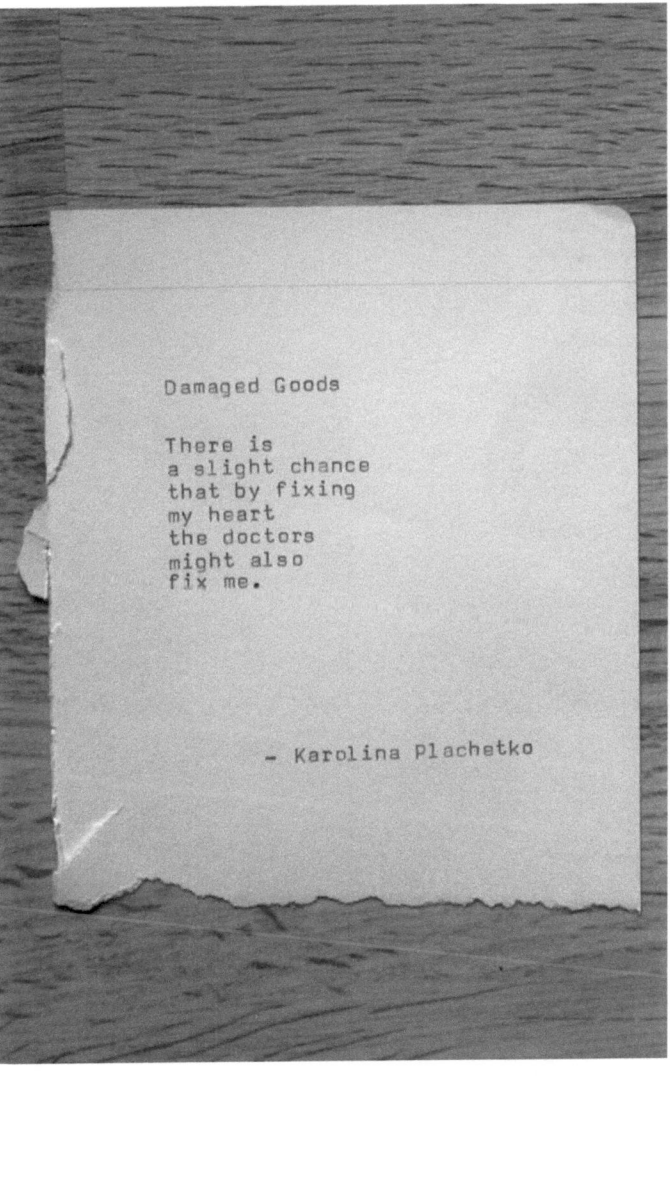

Damaged Goods

There is
a slight chance
that by fixing
my heart
the doctors
might also
fix me.

— Karolina Plachetko

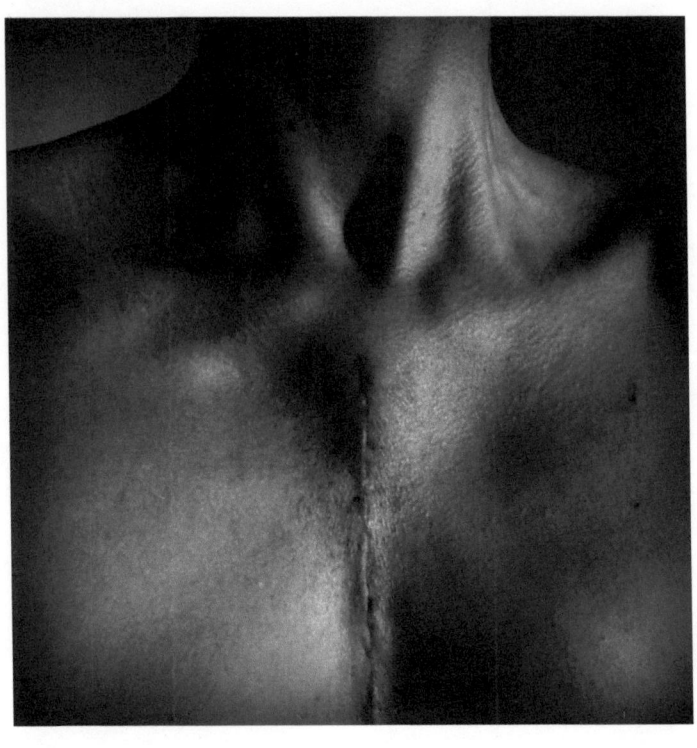

The Proposal

Can't we just skip
this whole
being insecure about
everything -
getting to know -
small talk -
part,

and simply love each other?

                - Karolina Plachetko

My Father's Hands

My hands are used and worn
like my father's.
I look at them and wonder,
sometimes, will he ever
~~hed~~ hold them again?
Will he remember them,
or me?
I look at my hands carefully:
a little wrinkled by now,
the nails too short and always
busy,
the knuckles bigger than those
of beautiful women,
my palms, oh my palms,
they built a tree house when I
was younger,
my fists punched a boy after he
kissed me, and when I'm nervous
my hands change their color like
a mood ring.
The limes and calluses will
remember when my father will
start to forget.

　　　　　　　　— Karolina Plachetko

Those Memories

Oh those memories.
Decent reminders of fragrance and
beauty.
And the summer.
What haven't we promised back then
when we were young.
Youth.
Our misery.
And now look at us.
The routine of every day life
kept its promise.
We're lonely when we hold each
other's hand.
We're broken in each other's eyes.
And the more we seek to remember
the more we drown.
In those memories
we're not allowed to keep
alive
anymore.

                    - Karolina Plachetko

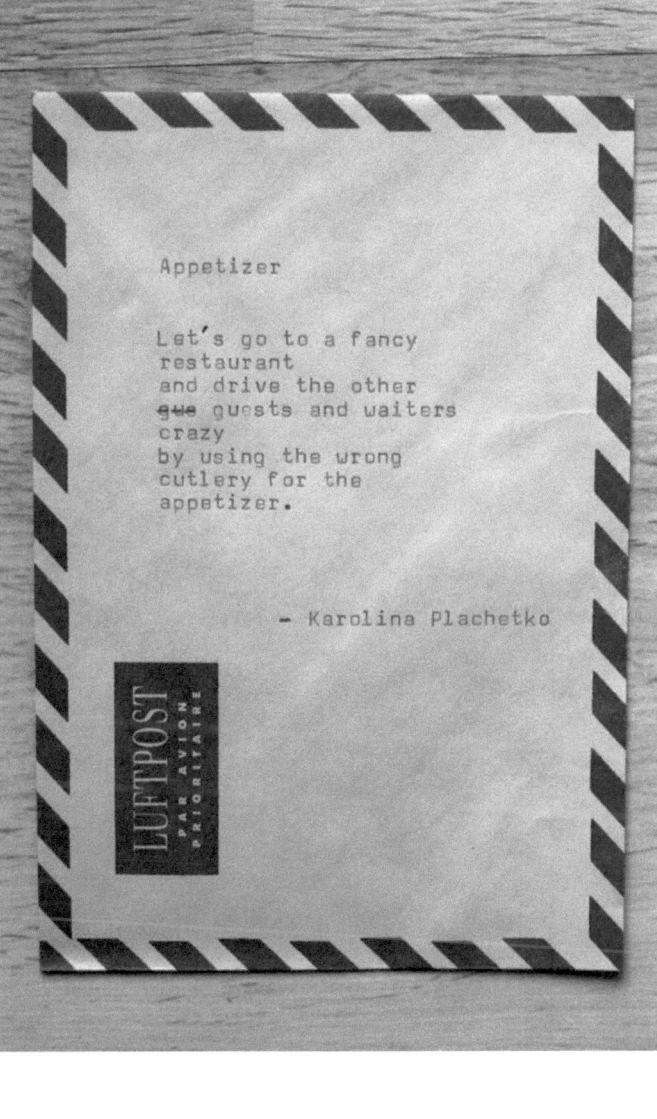

Appetizer

Let's go to a fancy
restaurant
and drive the other
~~que~~ guests and waiters
crazy
by using the wrong
cutlery for the
appetizer.

— Karolina Plachetko

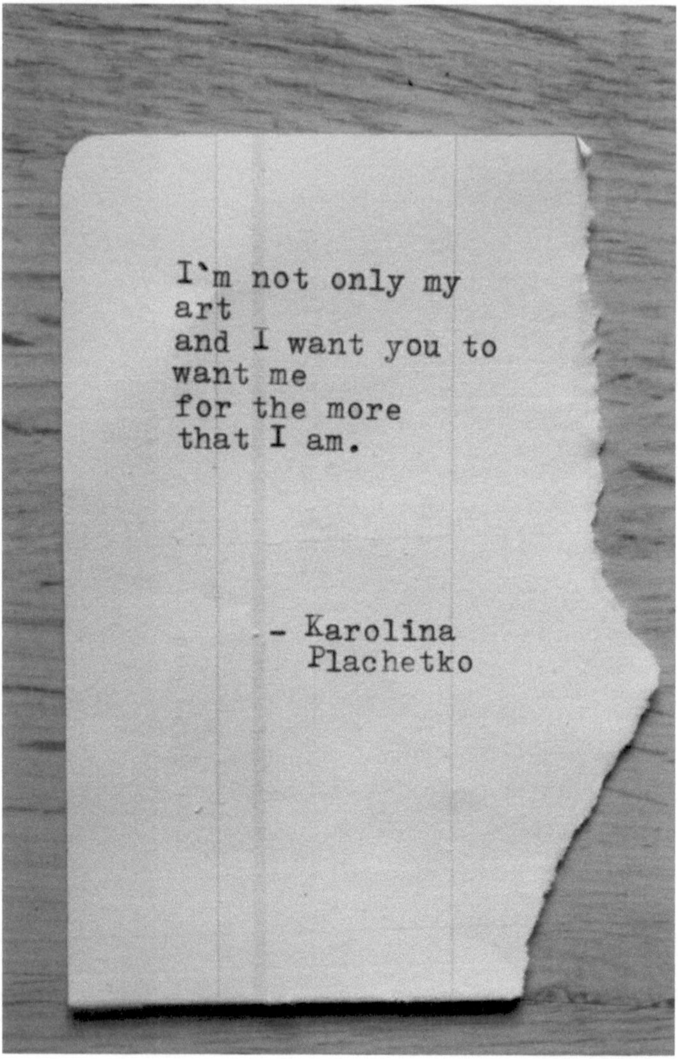

I'm not only my
art
and I want you to
want me
for the more
that I am.

        - Karolina
          Plachetko

We threw stones at the ~~pigeons~~
pigeons and ran away from the
dogs.
Someone stole my bike,
you laughed at my funny face.
It was summer or ~~was~~ something
in between,
the nights and kisses open
24 hours.
I was young and you were a
mess.

We promised never to forget.

        - Karolina Plachetko

Pandora

I watch your body move
the scars
the shrines
the sinkings

you catch me
and leave me
drowning
devastated
like the shark
once sharpened and slinky
now cut in half
by fisher men
hunting only for profits

        - Karolina Plachetko

Here I lay

Here I lay
crestfallen, unforgiven
the sinner
forbidden to confess

The room fills with light
the light I cannot see
for I am doomed now
~~dem~~ doomed
with my dishonesty

The forest park closes
the silence is framed
the night sneakily lenghtens
and here I lay

- Karolina Plachetko

Ergebnisse 070820 nach Themen.xls 12.09.2007

Songs without
Words

I still
ache
for you.

— Karolina
Plachetko

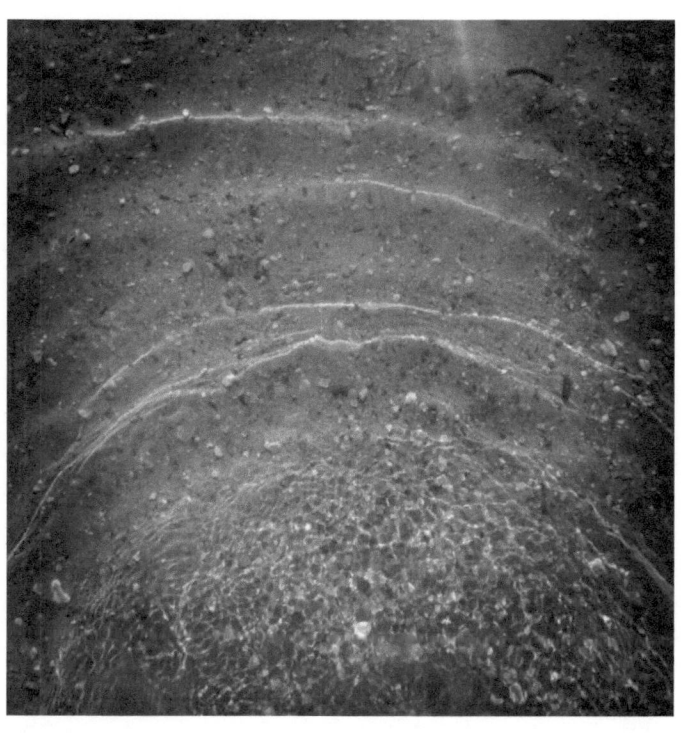

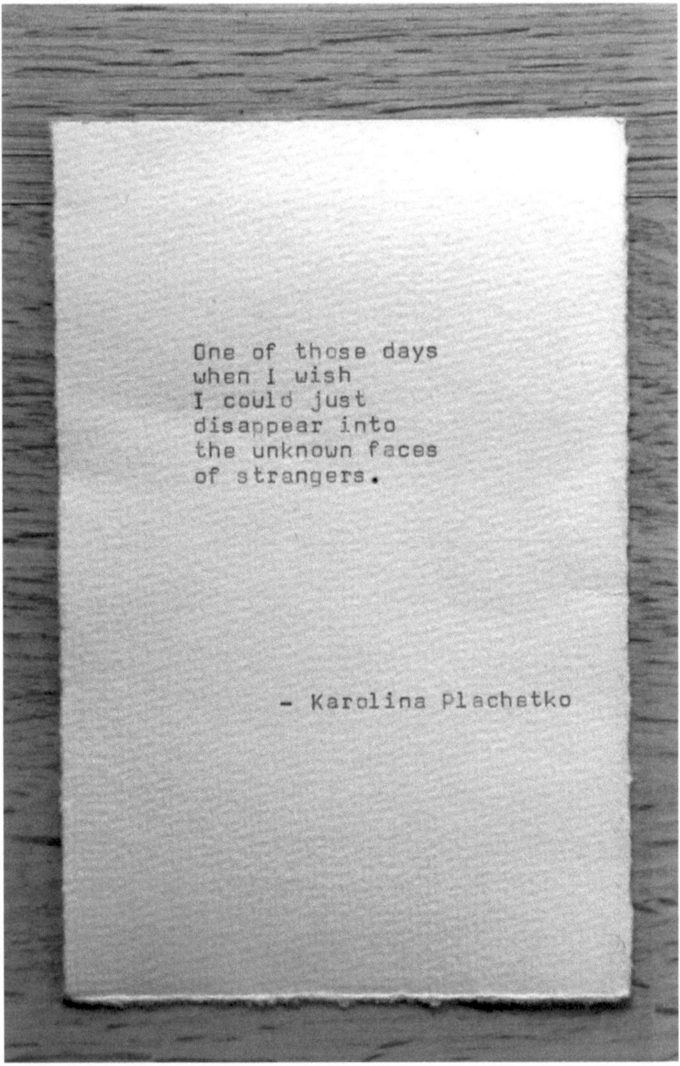

One of those days
when I wish
I could just
disappear into
the unknown faces
of strangers.

— Karolina Plachetko

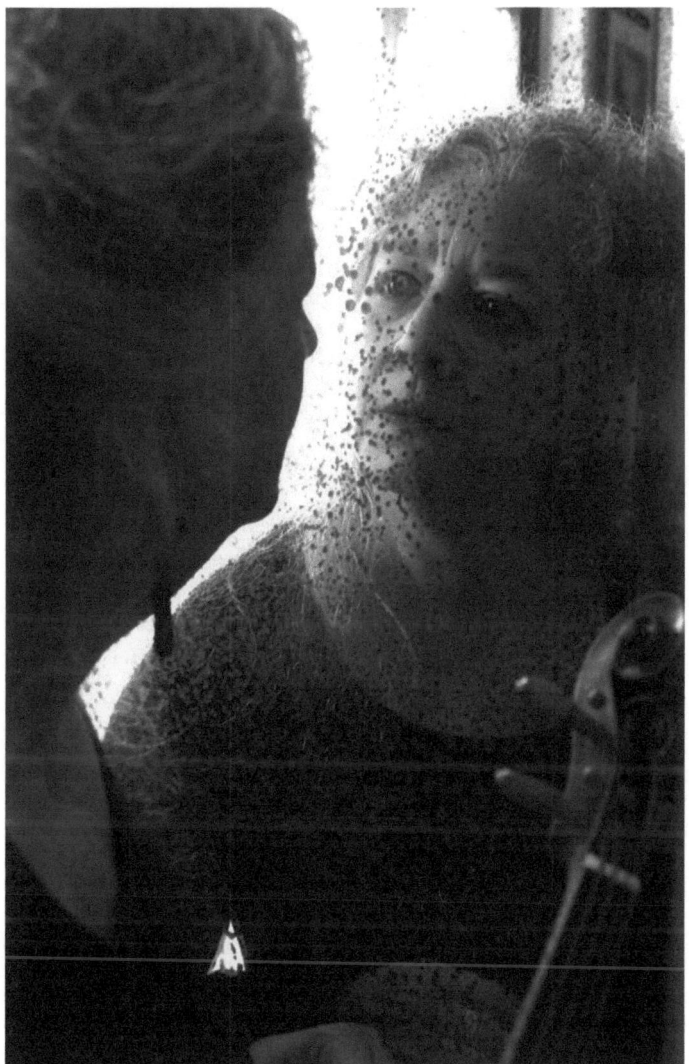

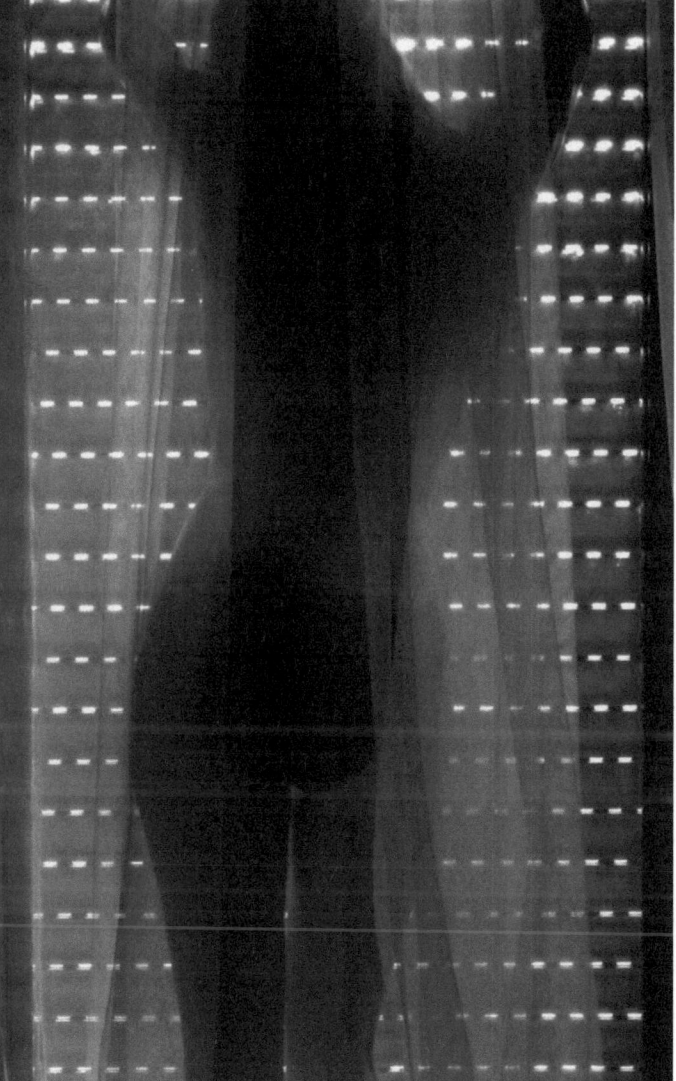

Confession of Age

The sun bathes in your
skin.

Right there,
under your chin.

Where the moon
covers up
all
the wrinkled,
~~lesy~~ lossy and
resolving
marks
of your
incoherent imagination.

          - Karolina Plachetko

Don't force me to remember.
My love, don't try.
It's long gone.
It's all lost.
And so am I.

Köln, 11.09.2009
Go/Ke

- Karolina Plachetko

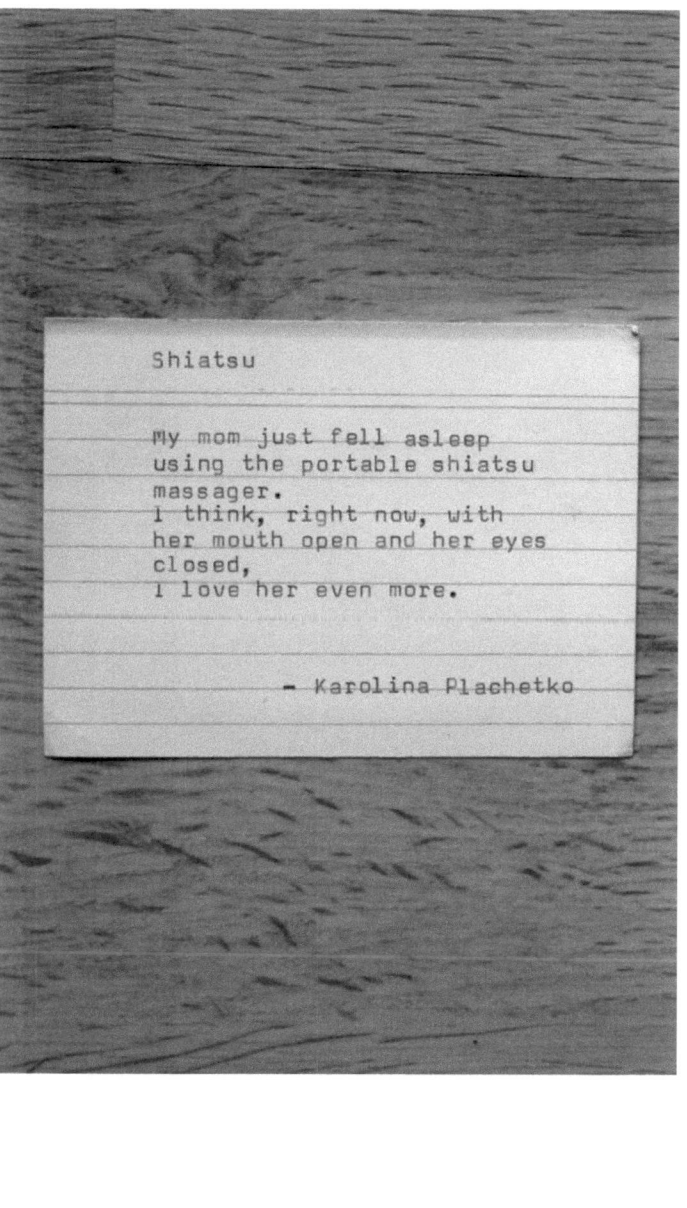

Shiatsu

My mom just fell asleep
using the portable shiatsu
massager.
I think, right now, with
her mouth open and her eyes
closed,
I love her even more.

                    — Karolina Plachetko

Sustenance

Don't try to fix me,
because I'm not the one
who's broken.

I know you feel at home
within your insecurity,
but I will no longer ask you
for an invitation.

~~One should leave off~~
~~with an appetite,~~
so they say.
And I think
you're in need for a diet.

             - Karolina Plachetko

8   To Come Uninvited

9

10 The moon is a crescent
    ~~tonight.~~

11 The slight memory
    of silent fullness.

12 ~~The witness~~

13 of my ridiculous expectations.

14 ~~I wish~~

15 you would want me
    to come with you.

16 ~~I wish~~

17 you would ask me
    to come with you.

18

19 I can't, not now, and
    maybe never.
    ~~But if only you spoke~~
    the words
    and voiced your invitation.

                    — Karolina Plachetko

Summer Son

you don't need
to follow
what ~~ei~~ is ~~et~~ set
to be the way
you just lie there
and watch me burn
in the hot and spicy
summer
of your eye

        — Karolina Plachetko

Piece of Good
Advice

Marina Abramović
once said,
don't fall in love
with another
artist.
She was so right.

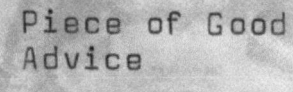

- Karolina
  Plachetko

Pure

I want to do things with my own
hands. Not only touch these things
or eventually stroke with my fingers
over them. I need to make these
things, i need to build them, to
restore them from my memory, to
expand them from my imagination.
i long my hands to bring these
things into life, piece by piece,
layer by layer, like a ceramist
who does pottery, like a butcher
who prays ~~before he slaughters the~~
~~meat,~~ for the dying soul before he
slaughters the meat. I want to be
at once ~~delistee and harsh deliv~~
delicate and harsh in what i do
with my hands. I want to feel every
bit of life between a feather and
a rock slipping, dripping, passing
through my fingers. i want to spend
uncountable hours working on these
things. i want to feel my fingers,
knuckles and ~~pl eale~~ palms ache
and burn and crash eventually. I
want to feel what i do, so my hands
can do ~~wje~~ what i feel.
Unleashed, unbound, unciphered,
pure. Pure.

                    - Karolina Plachetko

Carnival Parade

Think of me when I am burried
Think of me when I'm alive
Don't rush your love into a
hurry
Don't rush your love into a
thrive
Touch me when I am naked
Touch me when I am clean
Long before I turn into
sacred
Long before my body's steam
Hold me through the one last
morning
Hold me closer than it seems
Your kiss will be my
goodbye warning
Your kiss will lightly
be redeemed

                    _ Karolina Plachetko

The Release

In the hybrid chambers of my
soul,
a thought, a dream, a picture
rises,
compassionate and vicious both,
claiming its demand,
its purpose.
Forbidden there to be,
it steals itself from duty
and yawns into my inner eye,
way~~thr~~ through into my heart.
I cannot change the one I am,
furthermore cannot pretend
to keep my ~~dist~~ distance.
You will neither find a cure to
fix me,
nor will you bind my longing,
the unexpected thrist of passion.
Don't try to solve the mystery
occuring first in secret gardens.
It is not meant to be
lost sons returning to their
fathers.

                — Karolina Plachetko

Blades of grass

Moments ago you splashed
your younger sister and
your skin smelled of warm
water and ~~child~~ childhood
games.
And then, afterwards, you sat
next to me and started
talking. Easily we fooled
each other into the promises
of a summer still to
come.
And I remembered what it
once was like to crash
and burn on afetrnoons like
this.
But you were still a boy
then and I refused my
sudden urge to touch you.

                    - Karolina Plachetko

Resemblance

Would you just be my man?
With all your imperfections
matching mine,
and the faked smile
when you're feeling lost?

I would bed your head
in my lap then,
and stroke your hair
while telling you
all those stories
I've never told
anyone before.

- Karolina Plachetko

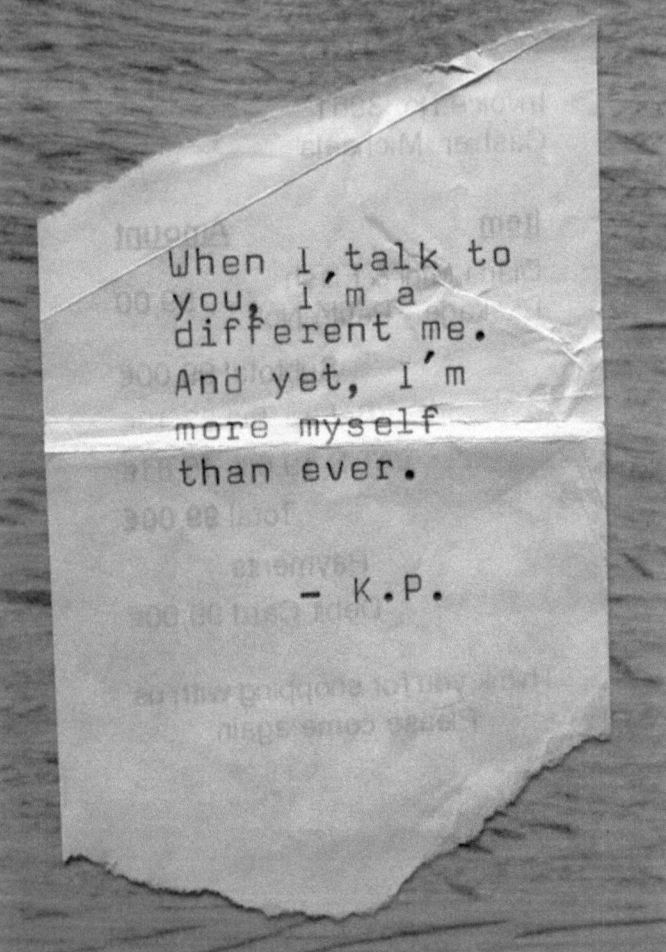

When I talk to
you, I'm a
different me.
And yet, I'm
more myself
than ever.

                - K.P.

The Muse

I will
never be
the inspiration
she was
for you.

— Karolina Plachetko

We ate grapes and passion
fruits.
One morning by the beach.
But we're not that young
anymore.
And I was never a beauty.

- Karolina Plachetko

Morning Stories

On our way to school this morning,
my daughter and I came across a
bunch of 12 or 13 year old boys
also on their way to school.
Feeling all ~~eeuraged~~ courages in
the comfort of the croud and
within the hormonal changes of
puberty, one of the boys started
dancing towards me way too sexy
for his age while the others sang
"Hey, sexy lady...", dancing a
little too.

As they passed, ~~me~~ ~~ty~~ my ~~daugh~~
~~dauf~~ daughter looked at them and
then at me and aoked, "Mama, did
you see this?"
"I did. Pretty cool, huh?",
I answered.
"Yes, pretty cool, but a little
too sexy I think."

                    - Karolina Plachetko

Rancor and Loathing

In the essence of my longing
right before morning
I burn and my lips turn into
ashes
while the fire lingers on
I am not superior
I am not a better human
because of some good intentions
or the prosperity of my mind
Good will is useless
right before morning
and so is the essence of my
longing
remaining the most selfish
side
of the concept called surface
wherein everything is kept
hidden from the true
the altruistic of all emotions:
rancor and loathing

            — Karolina Plachetko

I'm tired.
Tired with nothing.
Tired with everything.
Tired with
the world
I've chosen to bear.

- Karolina Plachetko

Brown Buttons

Do you remember your first kiss ever?
I do. I was eight or nine and I had
a crush on my brother's best friend,
Rosario. He had these Italian dark
brown eyes and dark brown curled
hair too, and he was a little smaller
than me, and all the girls were crazy
about him. I was too but I never
~~telf~~ told anyone. But because he and
my brother were friends, Rosario
came by almost every single day. We
were crazy about cartoons and the
Ninja Turtles and about games kids
play, chasy and whatnot. And this
one afternoon after school he kissed
me, unexpected and sudden, in a
hurry almost, just like that.
A fast kiss on my lips.
I got pretty mad about him and I tore
his shirt as he tried to run away
from ~~his~~ the suprise of his first,
less innocent act of affection. I
think I even punched him, and I re-
member the color of his shirt,
turquoise with little brown buttons
he lost one during the quarrel.

Anne Vollmer, „Wir müssen frech sein, um uns Respekt zu verschaffen."

A few months ago I re-met him
because my brother got in touch
with him again.
Except for the age passing on his
face, Rosario de didn't change at
all, still Italian dark brown
eyes, still dark brown curled hair,
still a little smaller than me.
And the father of three children
now, the husband of a beautiful
wife.
After a little confused silence
we hugged and smiled at each other
and he said:

"You owe me a button."

"I know",
I replied and put one out of my
pocket.

                    - Karolina Plachetko

                              -2-

Frittered

What do I expect?
You don't even know me.

You don't know how blurry and crumbled I
look in the morning and how I tug the
blanket back on my face to hide it from
the cold sneaking in with the first blue
light of the dawning day.

You don't know how desperately I long for
my dreams to come back then, knowing they
are gone with my first glance out of the
window, missing them like one misses a
secret unrevealed.

You don't know how hot I need to shower to
heat up my limbs and my skin, because
otherwise I couldn't keep my teeth from
chattering and that awful sound would fill
the bathroom for minutes.

You don't know the way I look into the
mirror to see this face of mine staring
back at me like a familiar stranger who
lives inside my body without paying the
rent for years by now.

You don't know this first half of an hour
of my day. And this is always only the
beginning. What about the rest of it?

What about the rest of me?

                        — Karolina Plachetko

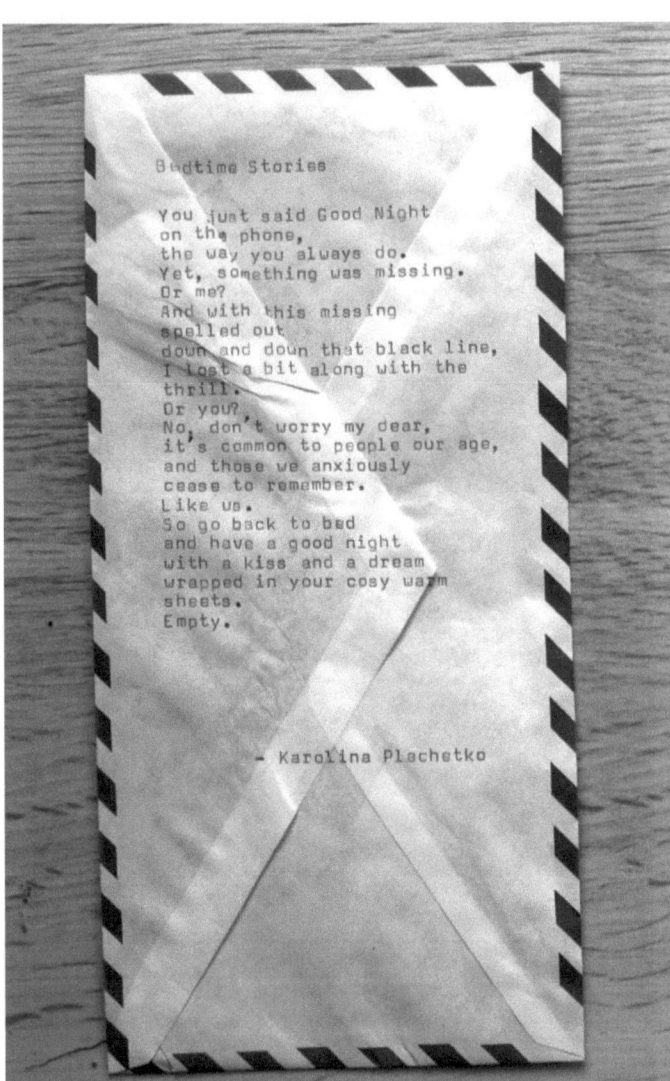

Bedtime Stories

You just said Good Night
on the phone,
the way you always do.
Yet, something was missing.
Or me?
And with this missing
spelled out
down and down that black line,
I lost a bit along with the
thrill.
Or you?
No, don't worry my dear,
it's common to people our age,
and those we anxiously
cease to remember.
Like us.
So go back to bed
and have a good night
with a kiss and a dream
wrapped in your cosy warm
sheets.
Empty.

                    - Karolina Plachetko

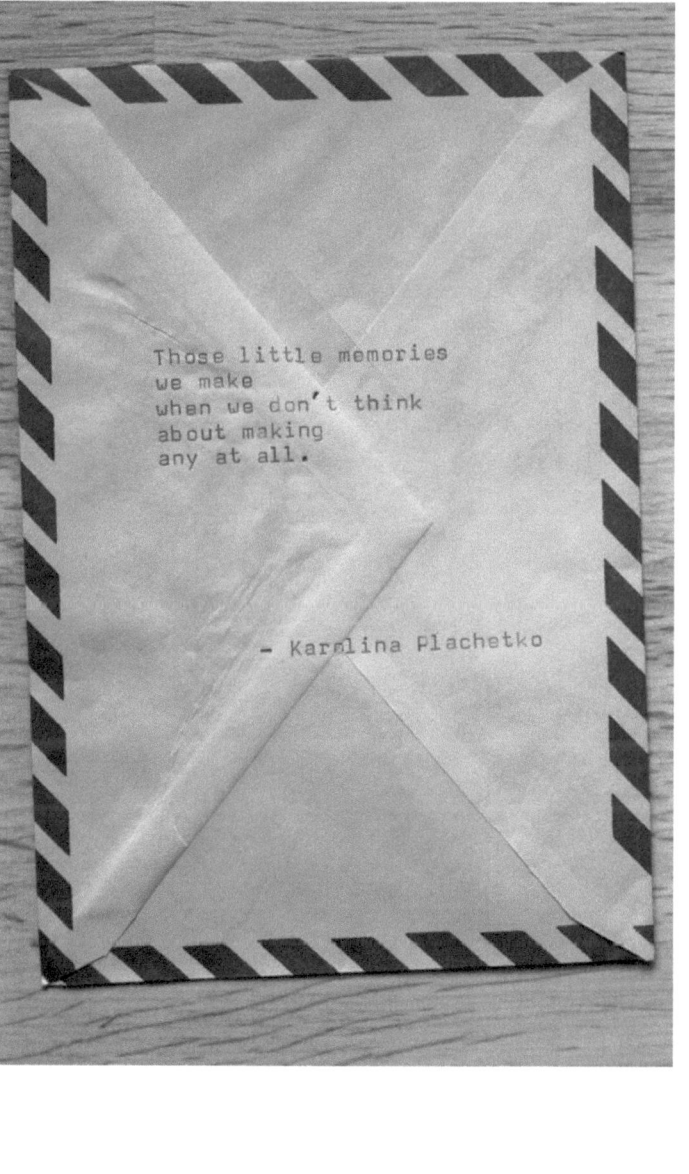

Those little memories
we make
when we don't think
about making
any at all.

— Karolina Plachetko

The Healing

I so wanted it to be us.
Lovers, you know.
Friends.
Those we talk to before
we talk to strangers.
Or not at all.

But you said,
there are no such things
like soul mates,
everybody is lonely,
we're all meant
to suffer from
this unexpected wound.

I think
I got lost
in yours.

                    - Karolina Plachetko

About the human heart

How many times
can a human heart love
before it turns into
a rotten piece of
arteries, fibres and flesh?

From human to human
this number may vary,
yet in the end
all human hearts die.

- Karolina Plachetko